A Little

Bit of

Positivity

A Little Bit of Positivity
Copyright © Aife Walsh 2022

ISBN: 978-1-3999-2144-2

For you, keep going

One day you're going to look back on this time and see the strength I see in you. I know there are days where it doesn't feel like you are strong because of those times you feel you're still struggling. Trust me when I say that with each day you keep going, you are becoming stronger and braver. You are growing with this strength and making steps of progress. Every storm will always pass, and the sun always finds a way back through the clouds. Keep holding onto hope. You've got this and everything will be okay very soon.

Look at how far you have come and look how much stronger you are today. Keep putting one foot in front of the other. You can keep going, day by day, step by step.

When the waves are feeling a little heavy and the wind a little strong, remind yourself that although you cannot change the direction of the wind, what you can always do, is adjust your sails to find a way that works for you.

If you're feeling a little lost and unsure of what your next step may be, know that it's okay. You don't have to have everything planned out just yet. Spend this time focusing on you and the things that you enjoy. This time is still valuable as you're growing and learning more about yourself every day. Be kind to yourself and trust that the right path will always find a way to you.

This feeling will pass. It may take time, but everything will feel okay very soon.

Repeat these positive affirmations out loud to yourself:

Recovery is possible.
Recovery is possible.
Recovery is possible.

On those days where you feel you're not good enough, read this message back and remind yourself of everything you have achieved just by being you. Look at where you are today and look how much you have been able to accomplish this year all on your own. I know there are days where you doubt yourself and feel a little out of place but trust me when I say that you are enough and good enough. I believe in you, and I hope you can begin to believe in yourself a little more too.

Try not to worry about what happened today. Remind yourself that you tried your best and that will always be enough.

The light is always there. Sometimes we need a little help finding it and that is always okay. Remember the sun is always there during the storms and the light will get through the darkness soon. Keep going.

I know you're doubting yourself and feel like you are doing everything wrong. Try and turn those negative thoughts into positive ones. These mistakes are what help us grow and learn. They guide us and allow us to become better versions of ourselves. These experiences are stepping-stones to a better path and you can only go up from here.

Take a moment to breathe.

Inhale. Exhale.

Inhale. Exhale.

You've got this.

Daily reminder

You are safe here and nothing can hurt you in this moment.

Sometimes we have to lose what we love in order to do what is best for us. With change comes growth and this is your new beginning.

Your steps of progress may be feeling hard to see but simply being here and taking each day one at a time, shows how strong you really are. You've had to go through so much and I am proud of you for everything you have overcome.

This year doesn't have to be about making changes or setting goals. You are on your own path and it is okay to take as much time as you need to get to where you want to be.

You are not alone. There will always be someone out there to help you through anything you are going through.

Try not to let yourself feel like you're not worthy of love and kindness. You are worthy and your life matters.

The right people who are meant to be in your life will always find a way to you.

If you are feeling anxious, remind yourself that you have it in you to overcome this next step. You are so brave and I know you can get through this.

You deserve happiness. Always follow your heart and try not to let the pressures around you move you away from what you need right now.

Breathe through the fear and know that you can get through this. You are so much braver than you think you are.

Repeat these positive affirmations out loud to yourself:

I am exactly where I need to be.
I am exactly where I need to be.
I am exactly where I need to be.

Never underestimate the importance you hold because there are so many amazing qualities unique to you that you, and only you, hold. There is no one else in this world quite like you.

You make the world a better place.

Always put your mental health first and take whatever time you need to look after yourself. Take a break if you start to notice moments that are feeling too much and overwhelming. As little as five minutes can make a huge difference to your mindset. Spend time on you and treat yourself with the same kindness you show to others.

You have the strength to keep going. You are so much stronger than you think you are.

Daily reminder

Better days are always ahead, and they are on their way to you. Hang in there.

It is always okay to try again. If you didn't succeed the first time, it doesn't make you a failure or any less capable. Standing back up and trying again shows so much strength, and I'm so very proud of you.

You are beautiful.

You are valued.

You are brave.

You are strong.

You are enough.

Take some time today to recognise how far you have come. It really has been the most challenging journey and you've been so brave.

It is always okay to let someone know how you're feeling. We all struggle with mental health and you're not a burden for reaching out for help. Someone will understand and listen whenever you're ready to talk.

The darkest nights show the brightest stars and the challenges you are facing now, will lead you to brighter and better days.

You are enough just as you are and there are so many great qualities about you that make you who you are. You do not need to change for anyone.

Each day you fight through the storms, they add up to something. They give you strength. This strength is going to grow and grow until you're in a place where it doesn't feel so hard to keep fighting. You are going to get to that place, and you are already halfway way there. Keep going.

It's okay if things didn't go the way that you hoped. You tried your best and there will always be another opportunity for you to use what you've learnt and come out stronger next time.

Every day you are making steps of progress.

Keep going.

One day at a time.

You can do this!

It takes a lot of strength to keep going. I see how hard you are trying, and I know it is feeling impossible right now. Please know that in time things will feel easier and you will not always be feeling this pain. Keep holding onto that little bit of hope, and when you are having a day where you feel it will not ever change, think back to where you were a year ago. You are here, you made it through, and you are fighting which is something to be proud of. Keep believing in yourself and never give up.

Be kind to yourself for all the progress you have already made. I know it's feeling hard to see, but you are doing so much better than you think you are.

Keep trusting in your journey because everything you have been hoping for will find a way to you very soon.

For each negative thought that crosses your mind, try to fight against it. You are not your thoughts and you are enough just as you are.

I know it feels like you're holding the weight of the world all on your own. The heaviness is building up to a point where it feels like things are never changing or improving. If there's one thing you take from this message, let it be hope. Hope for better days. They are there and everything is going to be okay.

Be kind to yourself, you are trying your best
and that will always be enough.

Repeat these positive affirmations out loud to yourself:

My strength is greater than any struggle.
My strength is greater than any struggle.
My strength is greater than any struggle.

Celebrate your wins today no matter how small you feel they may be. Whether you've got out of bed, made yourself a meal, spoken to a friend, read this quote, spent time outside, or got through the challenges of the day, I am proud of you. Not many people understand the strength it takes to achieve these wins and I know it's been difficult. Take some time today to recognise your progress because you are doing so well.

Daily reminder

The hard work you are doing each day will be worth it very soon.

A flower needs a little rain to grow and bloom. When the rain passes, you will bloom too and come out so much stronger.

Love yourself a little more because there is so much to love about you.

These challenges and hurdles are just temporary, and they won't last forever. Storms always pass and this one you're going through will too.

I know there's a lot going on in your life and it's feeling overwhelming. When it feels as tough as it is right now, it's always okay to put yourself first and say no to the pressures around you to do what's best for you. As hard as it is to say no, the people around you should understand, and your mental health and wellbeing should always come first.

Never be afraid to let the fear of failure stop you from following your dreams.

I can see the progress you're making and I'm so very proud of you. I know it's feeling hard to see your growth right now, but you are doing so much better than you think you are.

H.O.P.E

Hold

On

Pain

Ends

Daily reminder

Just because you're struggling and going through a tough time, doesn't mean you're failing.

Try not to let the pressures of society make you feel like you're not good enough. Being yourself is perfect enough and you will always be enough.

It's okay if you're struggling with all the changes that are happening in your life right now. Change can be hard and incredibly tough to go through. You're not alone in finding this difficult. Take each day as it comes and trust that things will start to settle and feel okay again very soon.

You can do anything that you set your mind to. You are brave enough. You are strong enough. You are capable enough. Never give up.

You have never lost a battle that has come your way. Keep fighting and remember how strong you really are.

I am proud of you for getting through another week. I know it's been hard, and you've faced so many challenges. Try not to doubt yourself because you are incredible.

Look how much you have achieved this year. You have been able to push on through when everything was shattering around you. I am proud of you.

You are doing your best to be okay. That takes strength some will never know. You really do have it in you to keep going. Keep believing in yourself because I believe in you.

Daily reminder

You are doing the best you can with what is going on in your life right now.

It is okay if you do not feel like you can give it your all. You are allowed to have days where you feel sad and let yourself feel your emotions. Sometimes we need those days and that will always be okay.

I hope you know that there are people in this world who care about you.

Repeat these positive affirmations out loud to yourself:

I am a warrior, and I can keep going.
I am a warrior, and I can keep going.
I am a warrior, and I can keep going.

Put your mental health first and take time today for self-care. Reach out for support, take a break, make a self-care box, meditate, switch off your phone and disconnect for a while. Do whatever is best for you and know that it's alright to take the time you need to look after yourself.

Change can be hard, and it often happens so fast. There will be days where you feel sad, and you miss the comfort you once had. However, change can also be beautiful, and the autumn leaves show us the beauty in letting things go.

By opening this book, you have taken a step to help yourself. The first step is often the hardest to make and I'm proud of you.

Focus on the step that's in front of you instead of the whole staircase. Each step is important progress even if it feels small. Keep going, one step at a time.

I hope it helps to know that what happened in your past, doesn't define you and it's okay to let that go and start again.

Be kind to yourself for the mistakes you think you have made. You are only human, and we all need to make mistakes to learn and grow.

It's going to be alright.

It's going to be alright.

Repeat these words.

It's going to be alright.

It's going to be alright.

Don't be afraid to let others see you vulnerable. It's always okay to cry and let your tears fall.

If today feels impossible, I want you to know that it is possible. If you look at the word 'impossible' it says, 'I'm possible'. You really can do this.

Daily reminder

You are strong enough to get through these difficult days and you can handle anything that comes your way.

What a year it has been. You have been through so much and I know at times it has felt impossible to keep going. I am proud of you for fighting through.

You may be wondering if you will ever be enough. You are already enough just as you are, and you don't need to change for anyone.

If you're feeling anxious today, keep reminding yourself that these worries and thoughts will pass. Breathe in and out. Take as much time as you need to look after yourself and remind yourself that everything is going to be okay.

There are not enough words for me to say how proud I am of you. Even when it felt like the world was against you, like nothing was ever on your side, you kept going. You never gave up hope that better days were on their way to you. It takes so much strength to keep fighting when so many doors are closing around you. The light is finally finding a way through the clouds that have been there for so long. I'm so very proud of you.

It's okay if you haven't figured it out yet. Roads are never a perfect straight-line. Your journey may twist and turn and there may be bumps along the way, but just like a road, there's always a way through. You will find your way through too.

You have it in you to keep going. I see this strength in you and I know you can keep fighting. You've already got this far and overcome the toughest battles which is incredible. You have so many good things coming your way. Hold onto that and keep pushing through. You will always make it through.

Today is going to be a good day. Go out there and smash it! You've got this.

Daily reminder

You will look back on this time and all the struggles you went through and thank yourself for never giving up.

Ground yourself. Deep breaths. Inhale. Exhale. Bring yourself back to the present moment to calm your mind. List five things you can see, smell, hear, taste and feel.

What can you see?

What can you smell?

What can you hear?

What can you taste?

What can you feel?

I know you're feeling a little lost and broken from being knocked down too many times. You will find your confidence and strength again. It will take time and there will be days where it comes and goes, but you are still growing every day and becoming a beautiful version of yourself.

Things can always change and get better. You might not be able to see the light through those dark days, but it's always there. You can get through this and you're never alone.

Repeat these positive affirmations out loud to yourself:

I am beautiful inside and out.
I am beautiful inside and out.
I am beautiful inside and out.

You are not behind in life. I know it feels like your path is a little different to those around you, but this doesn't mean you are failing. There is no timeline you need to follow. You are exactly where you need to be. I am very proud of where you are in your life right now and how much you've achieved over the years. You really are incredible! Always do what makes you happy and the rest will fall into place.

Take a moment to calm your mind and relax with box breathing.

Breathe in and count to four.
Hold your breath and count to four.
Exhale for four seconds.

Repeat three times.

Love yourself first and make sure your cup is full so you can be the best version of you.

Let go of the people who are holding you
back so you can become the best version of
you.

It's okay to be feeling how you're feeling. It really is okay. You will find your happiness, I promise you.

Endings are incredibly challenging and you're not alone in finding them difficult. Allow yourself to grieve for what you have lost and know that it's okay to cry. Give yourself the time you need and don't be afraid to reach out for help.

Spend some time today reflecting on three things you're proud of and celebrate them today. There is so much you've achieved, and you deserve a day to recognise them!

I want you to know that the world is a better place because you're in it. Never forgot your worth.

Allow yourself to sit with your anxious thoughts and work through them. As uncomfortable as it may feel, you are facing them head on and it will help them pass. Be present, focus on the thoughts and trust you can get through them.

Recovery is always possible and you will get there. It may not be a straight line and it may take time, but it is possible for you.

It's never too late to chase your dreams. It's never too late to take that first step. It's never too late to reach out for help. It's never too late to be who you want to be. It's never too late to try again. It's never too late. You still have time.

I hope it helps a little to know that you're not alone in finding this time of year difficult. Take each day one at a time and remember how strong you are.

Maybe this was all supposed to happen for you to see the world in a different light. You might not be where you want to be right now, but you are growing everyday which is going to help you get to where you need to be. Keep going.

Every day you are becoming a better version of yourself. You are moving forward and tomorrow is a new day.

A message from the author

Thank you for purchasing my book and supporting my work, it means so much to me. A lot of these messages I wrote during a really difficult time in my life and found the process so therapeutic. I began to share them on Instagram and quickly connected with other people who were going through similar experiences. It helped me so much to know that I wasn't alone in what I was going through, and I hope with this book, it has helped you find a little strength too.

Instagram
@Justalittlebitofpositivity

Etsy
Etsy.com/shop/alittlepositivityy